To

D1064035

The Power of a Praying® Woman

Text © 2005 Stormie Omartian.

POWER OF A PRAYING® trademarks and copyrights are licensed exclusively
by Harvest House Publishers, Eugene, Oregon. All rights reserved.

Published by DaySpring® Cards, Inc.

Siloam Springs, Arkansas 72761

www.dayspring.com

Design by Lecy Design

All rights reserved. No part of this publication may be reproduced, stored in a retrieval
system or transmitted in any form by any means—electronic, mechanical, photocopying,
recording, or any other—without the prior written permission of the publisher.

Scripture quotations are taken from the New King James Version.

Copyright © 1982, Thomas Nelson, Inc.

Used by permission. All rights reserved.

ISBN 1-59449-398-7

Made in China

*W*e need to pray about every aspect of our life in such a manner that it will keep us spiritually anchored and reminded of what God's promises are to us. This kind of prayer will keep us focused on who God is and who He made us to be. It will help us live God's way and not our own.

JANUARY 1

*A*rise, shine; for your light has come! And the glory of the Lord is risen upon you. For behold, the darkness shall cover the earth, and deep darkness the people; but the Lord will arise over you, and His glory will be seen upon you.

Isaiah 60:1-2

DECEMBER 31

*W*hen we pray about every aspect of our life, it will lift our eyes from the temporal to the eternal and show us what is really important. This kind of praying will give us the ability to distinguish the truth from a lie. It will strengthen our faith and encourage us to believe for the impossible. It will enable us to become the women of God we *long* to be and believe we *can* be.
Who among us doesn't need that?

*L*ord, move me into powerful ministry that will impact the lives of others for Your kingdom and Your glory. I humble myself under Your mighty hand. O God, knowing that You will lift me up in due time, I reach out for Your hand today so I can walk with You into the future You have for me.

DECEMBER 30

*L*ord, You have said in Your Word that whoever believes in You will have rivers of living water flowing from their heart (John 7:38). I believe in You, and I long for Your living water to flow in and through me today and every day that I'm alive.

For I know the thoughts that I think toward you, says the Lord, thoughts of peace and not of evil, to give you a future and a hope. Then you will call upon Me and go and pray to Me, and I will listen to you. And you will seek Me and find Me, when you search for Me with all your heart.

Jeremiah 29:11-13

DECEMBER 29

*E*very woman has needs. But many of us are guilty of looking to other people to meet them—especially the men in our lives. Too often we expect *them* to meet the needs that only God can fill. And then we are disappointed when they can't. We expect too much from *them* when our expectations should be in *God*.

JANUARY 4

*R*emember, my precious sister in the Lord, that walking with God doesn't mean there won't be obstacles. God's plan for *your* life won't happen without a struggle, however, so don't give up when times get tough. Just keep on doing what's right and resist the temptation to quit. Ask God to give you the strength and endurance you need to do what you have to do.

DECEMBER 28

*W*e will never be happy until we make *God* the source of our fulfillment and the answer to our longings. He is the *only* one who should have power over our souls.

JANUARY 5

*L*ord, I put my future in Your hands and ask that You would give me total peace about it. I don't want to be trying to secure my future with my own plans. I want to be in the center of *Your* plans, knowing that You have given me everything I need for what is ahead.

DECEMBER 27

*L*ord, I invite Your Holy Spirit to fill me afresh right now. Just as a spring is constantly being renewed with fresh water so that it stays pure, I ask You to renew me in that same way today.

JANUARY 6

God "is able to do exceedingly abundantly above all that we ask or think, according to the power that works in us" (Ephesians 3:20). He has more for you than you can imagine. Stay focused on God, and He will keep you in perfect peace as He moves you into the future He has for you.

DECEMBER 26

*I*f you're like me, you don't want to live the kind of life where you are barely hanging on. You don't want to merely eke out an existence, find a way to cope with your misery, or just get by. You want to have the abundant life Jesus spoke of when He said, "I have come that they may have life, and that they may have it more abundantly" (John 10:10).

$\mathscr{R}$emember that you are God's daughter and He loves you. As you *walk* with Him, you will become more like Him every day (1 John 3:1-3). As you *look* to Him, you will be "transformed into the same image from glory to glory, just as by the Spirit of the Lord" (2 Corinthians 3:18).

DECEMBER 25

*W*henever you are disappointed because your needs are not being met, talk to yourself and say, "My soul, wait silently for God alone, for my expectation is from Him" (Psalm 62:5). Then tell God about all your needs and everything that is in your heart. Don't worry, He won't be surprised or shocked. He already knows. He is just waiting to hear it from you.

JANUARY 8

For I am persuaded that neither death nor life, nor angels nor principalities nor powers, nor things present nor things to come, nor height nor depth, nor any other created thing, shall be able to separate us from the love of God which is in Christ Jesus our Lord.

ROMANS 8:38-39

DECEMBER 24

$\mathcal{L}$ord, I realize I don't know how to pray as I need to, nor as often as I want to, but I invite You, Holy Spirit, to pray through me. Help me in my weakness. Teach me the things I don't know about You.

My grace is sufficient for you, for My strength is made perfect in weakness.

2 CORINTHIANS 12:9

JANUARY 9

$\mathcal{A}$lthough we live in a world where everything in our lives can change in an instant, and we can't be certain what tomorrow will bring, God is unchanging. You may already have lost your false sense of security, and this is good because God wants you to know that your only *real* security is found in Him.

DECEMBER 23

*W*e don't want to be women who hear the truth but seldom act in faith to appropriate it for our lives. We don't want to be forever grappling with doubt, fear, insecurity, and uncertainty. We want to live life *on* purpose and *with* purpose.

JANUARY 10

*D*o not remember the former things, nor consider the things of old. Behold, I will do a new thing, now it shall spring forth; shall you not know it? I will even make a road in the wilderness and rivers in the desert.

Isaiah 43:18-19

DECEMBER 22

We want to be connected to what God is doing on earth in a way that bears fruit for His kingdom. We want to have a sense of purpose in our lives. We want to abound in God's love and blessings. We want it all. All God has for us. But we can never achieve that quality of life outside the power of God. And then only as we pray.

Lord, help me to keep my eyes looking straight ahead and not back on the former days and old ways of doing things. I know You want to do something new in my life today. Help me to concentrate on where I am to go now and not where I have been. Release me from the past so I can move out of it and into the future You have for me.

DECEMBER 21

*L*ord, I am desperately aware of how much I need Your power to transform me and my circumstances. You paid a price for me so that I could be owned by You. You planned out a course for my life so that I could be defined by You. Help me to live like it.

One of the great mysteries of the Lord is how He can take the horrible, the tragic, the painful, the devastating, the embarrassing, and the ruinous experiences and memories of our lives and not only heal them, but use them for good. It's not that He will make you unable to recall them, but He will heal you so thoroughly from their effects that you no longer think about them with any pain.

DECEMBER 20

$\mathcal{W}$e don't want to spend our lives waiting to be delivered from all that limits us and separates us from God's best. We want to be set free *now*. Without transformation, how can we ever rise above our limitations and be God's instruments to reach the world around us? And that is what life is all about.

JANUARY 13

*L*ord, I release my past to You and everyone associated with it so You can restore what has been lost. Everything that was done to me or I have done which causes me pain, I surrender to You. May it no longer torment me or affect what I do today. Thank You that You make all things new and You are making me new in every way.

Then He who sat on the throne said, "Behold, I make all things new."

REVELATION 21:5

DECEMBER 19

I put all my expectations in You, Lord. I repent of the times I have expected other people or other things to meet my needs when I should have been looking to You. I know that You are the only one who can complete me because You are everything I need. All that I have ever wanted in my life can be found in You.

We have this treasure in earthen vessels, that the excellence of the power may be of God and not of us.

2 CORINTHIANS 4:7

JANUARY 14

*W*hether it's something that happened as long ago as your early childhood or as recently as yesterday, the past can keep you from moving into all God has for you. That's why He wants to set you free from it. And not only that, He wants to redeem and restore what has been lost or destroyed in your past and make it count for something important in your life.

God wants us to understand "what is the exceeding greatness of His power toward us who believe" (Ephesians 1:19). He wants us to know this power that raised Jesus "from the dead and seated Him at His right hand in the heavenly places, far above all principality and power and might and dominion, and every name that is named" (Ephesians 1:20-21).

JANUARY 15

*T*he Spirit Himself bears witness with our spirit that we are children of God, and if children, then heirs—heirs of God and joint heirs with Christ, if indeed we suffer with Him, that we may also be glorified together.

ROMANS 8:16-17

DECEMBER 17

When we live according to God's Word and by the power of His Holy Spirit, then we can trust that we are in the right place at the right time and that the Lord is working His perfect will in our lives. We can trust that He is moving us into the life of wholeness and blessing He has for us.

JANUARY 16

$\mathcal{L}$ord, may Your light so shine in me that I become a light to all who know me. May it be not I who live, but You who live in me. Make me to be so much like Christ that when people see me they will want to know You better.

I have been crucified with Christ; it is no longer I who live, but Christ lives in me; and the life which I now live in the flesh I live by faith in the Son of God, who loved me and gave Himself for me.

GALATIANS 2:20

DECEMBER 16

*L*ord, help me to remember to live not in my own strength, but by the power of Your Spirit living in me. Forgive me for the times I have forgotten to do that. Enable me to grow in the things of Your kingdom so that I can become a whole, properly functioning, contributing, productive child of Yours who moves forward in Your purpose for my life.

God both raised up the Lord and will also raise us up by His power.

1 CORINTHIANS 6:14

JANUARY 17

$\mathcal{P}$eople are drawn to light. We want them to be drawn to the light of the Lord in us. Jesus said, "I am the light of the world. He who follows Me shall not walk in darkness, but have the light of life" (John 8:12). Ask God to make you more like Christ so that everyplace you go people will stop you and say, "Tell me what you know." "What is this special thing you have?"

DECEMBER 15

The God of the Bible is the one, true, living God. And when we find *Him* and receive *Him*, His Spirit comes to dwell *in* us. By the power of His Spirit, He transforms us from the inside out and miraculously changes our circumstances and our lives.

JANUARY 18

*J*esus was *in* the world, but He was not a *part* of the world. He came to *touch* the world, but He never became *like* the world. He was separate from the world, yet He changed the world around Him. We must pray that we can find that balance too.

DECEMBER 14

He is a God who can be found. A God who can be known. A God who wants to be close to us. That's why He is called Immanuel, which means "God *with* us." But He draws close to us as we draw close to *Him* (James 4:8).

$\mathcal{L}$ord, help me to become separate from the world without becoming isolated from it or turning my back on it. Show me when I am not humble and help me to resist pride of any kind. Let my humility be a testimony of Your Spirit in me. May Your love manifested in me be a witness of Your greatness. Teach me to love others the way You do.

DECEMBER 13

*L*ord, I draw close to You today, grateful that You will draw close to me as You have promised in Your Word. I long to dwell in Your presence, and my desire is for a deeper and more intimate relationship with You.

Draw near to God and He will draw near to you.

JAMES 4:8

JANUARY 20

*W*hen we don't feel we have anything to give, God supplies it all. "God is able to make all grace abound toward you, that you, always having all sufficiency in all things, may have an abundance for every good work" (2 Corinthians 9:8). Pray that God will fill you with His good gifts to give to those He brings into your life.

DECEMBER 12

*I*f you have received the Lord, the answer to what you need is within you. That's because the Holy Spirit of God is within you, and He will lead you in all things and teach you everything you need to know. He will transform you and your circumstances beyond your wildest dreams if you will give up trying to do it on your own and let *Him* do it *His* way and in *His* time.

JANUARY 21

$\mathcal{G}$od's love can work miracles in your life and in the lives of people you touch. The love of God in you will grow and reproduce as you share it. Pray for God's love to be revealed in you as you reach out to the world around you.

A new commandment I give to you, that you love one another; as I have loved you, that you also love one another.

JOHN 13:34

*Y*ou long for the closeness, the connection, the affirmation that who you are is good and desirable. But God is the only one who can give all that to you all of the time.

JANUARY 22

*L*ord, I know that "he who doubts is like a wave of the sea driven and tossed by the wind" (James 1:6). I confess any doubt I have as sin before You, and I ask You to forgive me. I don't want to hinder what You want to do in me and through me because of doubt. Increase my faith daily so that I can move mountains in Your name.

DECEMBER 10

*L*ord, I want to know You in every way You can be known. Teach me what I need to learn in order to know You better. I want to know the truth about who You are, because I know that You are near to all who call upon You in truth (Psalm 145:18).

JANUARY 23

*W*hat prayer would you like to boldly pray in faith and see answered? What would you like to see accomplished in your life, or in the life of someone you know, that would take a prayer of great faith? Ask God to take that seed you have and grow it into a giant tree of faith so you can see these things come to pass.

DECEMBER 9

*Y*our deepest needs and longing will only be met in an intimate relationship with God. No person will ever reach as deeply into you as God will. No one can ever know you as well or love you as much. That insatiable longing for more that you feel, the emptiness you want those closest to you to fill, is put there by God so that *He* can fill it.

JANUARY 24

*E*ven when your faith seems small, you can still speak in faith to the mountains in your life and tell them to move, and God will do the impossible. You can pray for the crippled parts of your life to be healed and God will restore them. You can ask God to increase your faith and give you boldness to act on it, and He will do it.

But without faith it is impossible to please Him, for he who comes to God must believe that He is, and that He is a rewarder of those who diligently seek Him.

HEBREWS 11:6

DECEMBER 8

God, help me to set aside time each day to meet with You alone. Enable me to resist and eliminate all that would keep me from it. Teach me to pray the way You want me to. Help me to learn more about You.

Until now you have asked nothing in My name. Ask, and you will receive, that your joy may be full.

JOHN 16:24

JANUARY 25

$\mathcal{L}$ord, increase my faith. Teach me how to "walk by faith, not by sight" (2 Corinthians 5:7). Give me strength to stand strong on Your promises and believe Your every word.

So Jesus said to them..."For assuredly, I say to you, if you have faith as a mustard seed, you will say to this mountain, 'Move from here to there,' and it will move; and nothing will be impossible for you."

MATTHEW 17:20

DECEMBER 7

*G*od wants us to want Him. And when we realize that it's Him that we want, we become free. We are free to identify the longings, loneliness, and emptiness inside of us as our signal that we need to draw near to God with open arms and ask Him to fill us with more of Himself.

JANUARY 26

We have no idea what great things God wants to do through us if we will just step out in faith when He asks us to. That's why He lets us go through some difficult times. Times when we feel weak and vulnerable. He allows certain things to happen so that we will turn to Him and give Him our full attention. It's in those times, when we are forced to pray in greater faith, that our faith grows stronger.

DECEMBER 6

God has so much to speak into your life. But if you don't draw apart from the busyness of your day and spend time alone with Him in quietness and solitude, you will not hear it. Jesus Himself spent much time alone with God. If anyone could get away with not doing it, surely it would have been Him. How much more important must it be for us?

JANUARY 27

*G*od takes the tiniest bit of faith we have and makes it grow into something big when we act on it. The Bible says that "God has dealt to each one a measure of faith" (Romans 12:3). We already have some faith to start with. When we step out in that faith, God *increases* our faith. In other words, acting in faith begets more faith.

DECEMBER 5

*L*ord, You have said, "If anyone thirsts, let him come to Me and drink" (John 7:37). I thirst for more of You because I am in a dry place without You. I come to You this day and drink deeply of Your Spirit.

JANUARY 28

*B*ut sanctify the Lord God in your hearts, and always be ready to give a defense to everyone who asks you a reason for the hope that is in you, with meekness and fear; having a good conscience, that when they defame you as evildoers, those who revile your good conduct in Christ may be ashamed. For it is better, if it is the will of God, to suffer for doing good than for doing evil.

1 PETER 3:15-17

DECEMBER 4

*P*rayer can turn your life around, but it doesn't always happen the moment you utter your first words. It may take a time of continued prayer before you actually see the scenery change. This is normal, so don't give up. You will soon be heading full speed in a new direction.

JANUARY 29

*L*ord, help me to be a woman who speaks wisely, graciously, and clearly and never foolishly, rudely, or insensitively. Give me words that speak of the hope that is within me so I can explain my faith in a persuasive and compelling way. May the words I speak bring others into a fuller knowledge of You.

DECEMBER 3

*I*f you are sick, run to your Healer. If you can't pay your bills, run to your Provider. If you are afraid, run to your Hiding Place. If you are going through a dark time, run to your Everlasting Light.

JANUARY 30

When a wise woman speaks, her words are gracious. Ask God to create in you a clean heart so filled with His Spirit, His love, and His truth that it will overflow love, truth, and healing in your speech. Ask Him to help you find words that speak life to those around you.

DECEMBER 2

*L*ord, I know You are everywhere, but I also know that there are deeper manifestations of Your presence that I long to experience. Draw me close so that I may dwell in Your presence like never before.

Let us hold fast the confession of our hope without wavering, for He who promised is faithful.

HEBREWS 10:23

JANUARY 31

When a wise woman speaks, she doesn't talk too much. We have to be careful that we don't spend more time talking than is necessary (Ecclesiastes 5:3). We must ask God to make us wise in the amount of talking we do.

DECEMBER 1

I will pray the Father, and He will give you another Helper, that He may abide with you forever—the Spirit of truth, whom the world cannot receive, because it neither sees Him nor knows Him; but you know Him, for He dwells with you and will be in you.

JOHN 14:16-17

FEBRUARY 1

When a wise woman speaks, she tells the truth. When we don't speak the truth, we hurt others as well as ourselves.

Therefore, putting away lying, "Let each one of you speak truth with his neighbor," for we are members of one another.

EPHESIANS 4:25

NOVEMBER 30

*L*et God become your standard. Don't try to make something happen for yourself. Recognize that you *can't* make anything happen, but you can surrender your life to God and let *Him* make things happen.

When a wise woman speaks, she knows that timing is important. When things need to be said that are difficult for the hearer to receive, timing is everything. Certain words cannot be uttered with any success if the person listening is not open and ready to hear them.
It's important to discern that, and the only way to know for certain when to speak and what to say is to pray about it in advance.

NOVEMBER 29

*W*omen all over the world want to live fruitful lives. They want to dwell in God's grace while still obeying His laws. They want to be *unshakable* in God's truth yet *moved* by the suffering and needs of others. They want to know God in all the ways He can be known, and they want to be transformed by the power of His Spirit.

FEBRUARY 3

When a wise woman speaks, she gives a reason for the hope that is within her. The most important words we can speak are ones that explain our faith to anyone who asks or who will listen. We must be able to give a reason for the hope we have within us (1 Peter 3:15). We have to pray that God will help us become bold enough to clearly explain our faith in God.

NOVEMBER 28

*L*ord, I come humbly before You and ask You to cleanse my heart of every fault and renew a right spirit within me. Forgive me for thoughts I have had, words I have spoken, and things that I have done that are not glorifying to You or are in direct contradiction to Your commands.

FEBRUARY 4

*T*he best way to make sure that what comes out of our mouth is good is to put thoughts in our heart that are good. "Out of the abundance of the heart the mouth speaks" (Matthew 12:34). If we fill our heart with God's truth and God's love, that's what will come out.

*E*xamine your life closely. Be brave enough to say, "Lord, show me what is in my heart, soul, mind, spirit, and life that shouldn't be there. Teach me what I am not understanding. Convict me where I am missing the mark. Tear down my arrogance, pride, fear, and insecurities, and help me to see the truth about myself, my life, and my circumstances. Expose me to myself, Lord. I can take it. Enable me to correct the error of my ways. Help me to replace lies with truth and make changes that last."

FEBRUARY 5

*M*ost assuredly, I say to you, he who believes in Me, the works that I do he will do also; and greater works than these he will do, because I go to My Father. And whatever you ask in My name, that I will do, that the Father may be glorified in the Son. If you ask anything in My name, I will do it.

JOHN 14:12-14

NOVEMBER 26

*I*f you are hesitant to let the Lord expose your heart because of what He might reveal, then ask Him to give you the courage you need. In order to see positive changes happen in your life you have to be open to the cleansing and stretching work of the Holy Spirit.

FEBRUARY 6

$\mathcal{T}$he greatest blessings will come to you when you ask God to use you to touch the lives of others.

He who has a generous eye will be blessed, for he gives of his bread to the poor.

PROVERBS 22:9

NOVEMBER 25

$\mathcal{L}$ord, I know that You are "gracious and merciful, slow to anger and of great kindness" (Joel 2:13). Forgive me for ever taking that for granted.

*L*ord, show me what You want me to do today to be a blessing to others around me. Specifically, show me how I can serve my family, my friends, my church, and the people whom You put in my life. I don't want to get so wrapped up in my own life that I don't see the opportunity for ministering Your life to others.

NOVEMBER 24

*C*onfession gets sin out in the open before God. When you confess your sin, you're not informing God of something He doesn't know. He already knows. He wants to know that *you* know.

$\mathcal{I}$f you love God, you will love people and be motivated to do whatever you can to help them. Prayer is a good place to start.

Let us not love in word or in tongue, but in deed and in truth.

1 JOHN 3:18

NOVEMBER 23

*L*ord, I realize that You are a God who "knows the secrets of the heart" (Psalm 44:21). Reveal those to me if I am not seeing them. Show me any place in my life where I harbor sin in my thoughts, words, or actions that I have not recognized.

*P*rayer is the greatest gift we can give to anyone. Of course, if someone needs food, clothes, and a place to live, those needs must be met. But in giving that way, we mustn't neglect to pray for them as well. Material things are temporary, but our prayers for another person can affect them for a lifetime.

NOVEMBER 22

God forgives *every time* you confess sin before Him and fully repent of it. "Blessed is he whose transgression is forgiven, whose sin is covered" (Psalm 32:1). You can turn things around in your life when you turn to the Lord and repent.

FEBRUARY 10

$\mathcal{A}$s each one has received a gift, minister it to one another, as good stewards of the manifold grace of God. If anyone speaks, let him speak as the oracles of God. If anyone ministers, let him do it as with the ability which God supplies, that in all things God may be glorified through Jesus Christ, to whom belong the glory and the dominion forever and ever. Amen.

1 PETER 4:10-11

NOVEMBER 21

*L*ord, show me the truth about myself so that I can see it clearly. Examine my soul and expose my motives to reveal what I need to understand. I am willing to give up meaningless and unfruitful habits that are not Your best for my life. Enable me to make changes where I need to do so.

FEBRUARY 11

*L*ord, help me to serve You the way You want me to. Reveal to me any area of my life where I should be giving to someone right now. Open my eyes to see the need. Give me a generous heart to give to the poor. Help me to be a good steward of the blessings You have given me by sharing what I have with others. Use me to touch the lives of others with the hope that is in me.

NOVEMBER 20

*L*earn to confess and repent quickly so that the death process that is set in motion each time we violate God's rules is not given time to do it's full damage, "for the wages of sin is death" (Romans 6:23).

Beloved, if our heart does not condemn us, we have confidence toward God. And whatever we ask we receive from Him, because we keep His commandments and do those things that are pleasing in His sign.

1 JOHN 3:21-22

FEBRUARY 12

God will use your abilities and talents to touch others powerfully. When your heart is to give to others from what God has given to you, He will enable you to do that. Giving to God and to other people is such a vitally important part of our life on this earth that we can never achieve all we want to see happen in our lives if we're not doing that. It's a major factor in realizing the complete purposes of God for us.

NOVEMBER 19

$\mathcal{L}$ord, I pray that You will "have mercy upon me, O God, according to Your loving kindness; according to the multitude of Your tender mercies, blot out my transgressions. Wash me thoroughly from my iniquity, and cleanse me from my sin" (Psalm 51:1-2).

FEBRUARY 13

*L*ord, help me to grow in fear and reverence of You so that I may please You and escape the plans of evil for my life. Thank You that those who fear You will never lack any good thing.

The secret of the Lord is with those who fear Him, and He will show them His covenant.

PSALM 25:14

NOVEMBER 18

$\mathcal{A}$sk God every day to show you where your heart is not clean and right before Him. Don't let anything separate you from all God has for you.

If we confess our sins, He is faithful and just to forgive us our sins and to cleanse us from all unrighteousness.

1 JOHN 1:9

*G*od wants you to walk with Him and talk with Him and have the kind of relationship with Him where He shares Himself with you and tells you things you didn't know before and wouldn't know unless He revealed them to you. When you get close enough and quiet enough, He will whisper a secret to your heart and it will change your life. In that moment, any fear you have will be gone. Ask God to speak to you today.

NOVEMBER 17

Lord, "create in me a clean heart...and renew a steadfast spirit within me. Do not cast me away from Your presence, and do not take Your Holy Spirit from me" (Psalm 51:10-11). Make me clean and right before You. I want to receive Your forgiveness so that times of refreshing may come from Your presence (Acts 3:19).

FEBRUARY 15

$\mathcal{T}$he more you get to know the Lord and understand who He is, the more you will reverence Him and fear His displeasure. This is called the fear of the Lord, and it makes you want to obey Him. It's what draws you closer to God and increases your longing for more of Him. When you have the fear of the Lord, you fear what your life would be like without Him.

NOVEMBER 16

I acknowledged my sin to You, and my iniquity I have not hidden. I say, "I will confess my transgressions to the Lord," and You forgave the iniquity of my sin.

PSALM 32:5

FEBRUARY 16

*L*ord, show me where I allow fear to take root and help me to put a stop to it. Take away any fear of rejection and all fear of man from within me and replace it with the fear of the Lord.

NOVEMBER 15

*O*ften we don't recognize the unforgiveness that is in us. We *think* we are forgiving, but we really aren't. If we don't ask God to reveal our unforgiveness to us, we may never get free of the paralyzing grip it has on our lives. A big part of making sure our lives are clean and right before God has to do with forgiving other people. We can never move into all God has for us unless we do.

FEBRUARY 17

$\mathcal{T}$he things of the world often make us afraid. What kind of input are you receiving from the world? Is any of it causing fear in you? Do whatever you can to stay close to God. Fear disappears in the presence of the Lord.

There is no fear in love; but perfect love casts out fear, because fear involves torment. But he who fears has not been made perfect in love.

1 JOHN 4:18

NOVEMBER 14

$\mathcal{L}$ord, help me to be a forgiving person. Show me where I am not. Expose the recesses of my soul so I won't be locked up by unforgiveness and jeopardize my future. If I have any anger, bitterness, resentment, or unforgiveness that I am not recognizing, reveal it to me and I will confess it to You as sin.

*L*ord, guard my heart and mind from the spirit of fear. What I am afraid of today is (name anything that causes you to have fear). Take that fear and replace it with Your perfect love.

NOVEMBER 13

*I*t's very easy to have unforgiveness toward family members because they are with us the most, know us the best, and can hurt us the deepest. But for those very same reasons, unforgiveness toward one of them will bring the greatest devastation to our lives. That's why forgiveness must start at home.

FEBRUARY 19

$\mathcal{W}$e must look to God for approval and acceptance and not to people. If God does not have the first place in our hearts, we are constantly fearing man.

The fear of man brings a snare, but whoever trusts in the Lord shall be safe.

PROVERBS 29:25

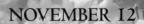

NOVEMBER 12

*I*t is very important to make sure you have forgiven your parents. The Bible is crystal clear about this issue. The fifth of the Ten Commandments says, "Honor your father and your mother, that your days may be long upon the land which the Lord your God is giving you" (Exodus 20:12). If you don't honor them it will shorten your life. And you can't fully honor them if you haven't forgiven them.

FEBRUARY 20

*T*here are two kinds of fear: godly and ungodly. We must pray that we live in godly fear, which is good, and not give place to ungodly fear, which is torment. One of the most common types of ungodly fear is the fear of man, or a fear of rejection. It's a trap we can fall into without ever realizing it. In order to protect ourselves from it, we have to care more about what *God* says than what anyone else says.

NOVEMBER 11

*L*ord, make me to understand the depth of Your forgiveness toward me so that I won't hold back forgiveness from others. I realize that my forgiving someone doesn't make them right; it makes me free. I also realize that You are the only one who knows the whole story, and You will see justice done.

FEBRUARY 21

*L*ord, You are my light and my salvation. You are the strength of my life. Of whom, then, shall I be afraid? Even though an entire army may surround me and go to war against me, my heart will not fear (Psalm 27:1-3). Free me from ungodly fear, for I know that fear is never of You.

*J*ust because we confess our unforgiveness toward someone one day doesn't mean we won't have unforgiveness in us the next. That's why forgiveness is a choice we must make *every* day. We *choose* to forgive whether we feel like it or not. It's a decision, not a feeling.

FEBRUARY 22

$\mathcal{G}$od does not want us to live in fear. Fear does not come from Him. It's the world that teaches us to fear. The things we see in movies, videos, newspapers, and books make us afraid. The enemy can make us afraid of everything, including our future. Worrying that something we fear is going to happen wears us down. But we don't have to be tormented by fear. God wants us to be free of it.

NOVEMBER 9

If we have any bitterness or unforgiveness, it's always our fault for not choosing to let it go. It's our responsibility to confess it to God and ask Him to help us forgive and move on with our lives.

FEBRUARY 23

*I*s anyone among you sick? Let him call for the elders of the church, and let them pray over him, anointing him with oil in the name of the Lord. And the prayer of faith will save the sick, and the Lord will raise him up. And if he has committed sins, he will be forgiven. Confess your trespasses to one another, and pray for one another, that you may be healed. The effective, fervent prayer of a righteous man avails much.

JAMES 5:14-16

NOVEMBER 8

*L*ord, help me to forgive myself for the times I have failed. And if I have blamed You for things that have happened in my life, show me so I can confess it before You.

$\mathcal{L}$ord, I want everything I do to be glorifying to You. Help me to be a good steward of the body You have given me. I know that my body is the temple of Your Holy Spirit, who dwells in me. Help me to fully understand this truth so that I will keep my temple clean and healthy. Help me not to mistreat my body in any way. Teach me how to properly care for my health.

NOVEMBER 7

*W*e don't tend to think of ourselves as unforgiving people. Irritated maybe, but not unforgiving. But we have to remember that our standards are much lower than God's, and therefore we often don't see where we need to forgive. Ask God to reveal any unforgiveness you have toward a family member.

The motivation for what we do in the area of body care is very important. It will affect how successful we are. If we eat right and engage in proper exercise for the purpose of being a more vital, healthy, energetic, and useful servant of the Lord, this has eternal consequences and you are more likely to stick with it.

Therefore, whether you eat or drink, or whatever you do, do all to the glory of God.

1 CORINTHIANS 10:31

NOVEMBER 6

*O*ur forgiving someone doesn't depend on them admitting guilt or apologizing. If it did, most of us would never be able to do it. We can forgive no matter what the other person does.

FEBRUARY 26

*L*ord, only You know the way You created me. Give me a solid ability to be disciplined about what I eat and drink and how I exercise. Enable me to discipline my body and bring it into subjection (I Corinthians 9:27).

NOVEMBER 5

Lord, remind me to pray for those who hurt or offend me so that my heart will be soft toward them. I don't want to become hard and bitter because of unforgiveness. Make me a person who is quick to forgive.

Judge not, and you shall not be judged. Condemn not, and you shall not be condemned. Forgive, and you will be forgiven.

LUKE 6:37

FEBRUARY 27

God wants us to live in balance and temperance and to take care not to abuse our body in any way. He wants us to glorify Him in the care of our bodies because we are the temple of His Holy Spirit.

For we know that if our earthly house, this tent, is destroyed, we have a building from God, a house not made with hands, eternal in the heavens.

2 CORINTHIANS 5:1

NOVEMBER 4

*F*orgiveness is never easy. But sometimes it feels downright impossible in light of the devastating and horrendous pain we have suffered. If you have a hard time forgiving someone, ask God to help you.

*L*ord, I thank You that You are the Healer, I look to You for my healing whenever I am injured or sick. I pray that You would strengthen and heal me today. I know that in your presence is where I will find healing. In Your presence I can reach out and touch You and in turn be touched by You.

NOVEMBER 3

If you can think of someone whom you find it hard to forgive, ask God to give you a heart of forgiveness for them. Pray for them in all the ways you can think of to pray. It's amazing how God softens our hearts when we pray for people. Our anger, resentment, and hurt turn into love.

FEBRUARY 29

*N*o matter how hard we try to do the right thing, we can't always prevent bad things from happening in our body. We should do the best we can to take care of ourselves, but we will still always need God to be our Healer.

NOVEMBER 2

*W*hen we forgive someone, it doesn't make them right or justify what they have done. It releases them into God's hands so *He* can deal with them. Forgiveness is actually the best revenge because it not only sets us free from the person we forgive, but it frees us to move into all God has for us.

My brethren, count it all joy when you fall into various trials, knowing that the testing of your faith produces patience. But let patience have its perfect work, that you may be perfect and complete, lacking nothing.

JAMES 1:2-4

NOVEMBER 1

Sometimes we don't forgive *ourselves* for things we've done, and so we give ourselves a lifetime of punishment for whatever we did or did not do. Sometimes we blame God for things that have happened. Ask God to show you if any of these things are true about you. Don't let unforgiveness limit what God wants to do in your life.

MARCH 2

Thank You, Lord, that You are near to all who call upon You, and You will fulfill the desire of those who fear You. Thank You that You hear my cries and will save me from any weakness that could lead me away from all You have for me (Psalm 145:18-19).

*L*ord, show me if I have any unforgiveness toward my mother or father for anything they did or did not do. I don't want to shorten my life by not honoring them and breaking this great commandment.

Jesus' temptation happened just before the greatest breakthrough in His life and ministry. It will happen before the greatest breakthrough in yours, too. Be ready for it. And remember that no matter how great the temptation is you face, "He who is in you is greater than he who is in the world" (1 John 4:4).

OCTOBER 30

$\mathcal{P}$eter asked Jesus, "Lord, how often shall my brother sin against me, and I forgive him? Up to seven times?" Jesus said to him, "I do not say to you, up to seven times, but up to seventy times seven" (Matthew 18:21-22). You may be able to think of someone you have to forgive 490 times a *day*, but the point is that God wants you to forgive as many times as it takes. He wants you to be a forgiving person.

MARCH 4

$\mathcal{T}$he best time to pray about temptation is *before* you fall into it. After the lure presents itself, resisting temptation becomes much more difficult. The model prayer Jesus taught us to pray as a matter of course is a good place to start.

Do not lead us into temptation, but deliver us from the evil one. For Yours is the kingdom and the power and the glory forever. Amen.

MATTHEW 6:13

OCTOBER 29

*W*e who have received Jesus have been forgiven a *large* debt. We have no right to be unforgiving of others. God says, "Be kind to one another, tenderhearted, forgiving one another, just as God in Christ forgave you" (Ephesians 4:32).

MARCH 5

$\mathcal{T}$he reason the enemy tempts you is because he knows of the great things God wants to do in your life, and he thinks you are dumb enough to give it all up for a few moments of pleasure. He knows that not only do *you* stand to lose from it, but other people will be hurt by your sin as well. When you see his trap, tell him you are not going to allow him to destroy your life or anyone else's.

OCTOBER 28

*E*verything we do in life that has eternal value hinges on two things: loving God and loving others. It's far easier to love God than it is to love others, but God sees them as being the same. One of the most loving things we can do is forgive.

MARCH 6

*L*ord, I pray I will have no secret thoughts where I entertain ungodly desires to do or say something I shouldn't. I pray that I will have no secret life where I do things I would be ashamed to have others see.

OCTOBER 27

God wants you to move into all He has for you. But if you don't forgive, you get stuck where you are and shut off God's work in your life. Forgiveness opens your heart and mind and allows the Holy Spirit to work freely in you. It releases you to love God more and feel His love in greater measure. Life is worth nothing without that.

MARCH 7

*T*herefore we also, since we are surrounded by so great a cloud of witnesses, let us lay aside every weight, and the sin which so easily ensnares us, and let us run with endurance the race that is set before us.

HEBREWS 12:1

OCTOBER 26

*L*ord, where there is distance between me and any family member because of unforgiveness, I pray You would break down that wall. Help me to forgive every time I need to do so. Where I can be an instrument of reconciliation between other family members who have broken or strained relationships, enable me to do that.

MARCH 8

*T*emptation can happen any time and often when you least expect it and are most susceptible. When it does happen, the danger is in thinking you can handle it alone. It's best to take it to God and confess it immediately, and then find someone trustworthy to pray with you about it.

Blessed is the man who endures temptation; for when he has been approved, he will receive the crown of life which the Lord has promised to those who love Him.

JAMES 1:12

OCTOBER 25

*L*ove your enemies, bless those who curse you, do good to those who hate you, and pray for those who spitefully use you and persecute you, that you may be sons of your Father in heaven.

MATTHEW 5:44-45

MARCH 9

*N*o temptation has overtaken you except such as is common to man; but God is faithful, who will not allow you to be tempted beyond what you are able, but with the temptation will also make the way of escape, that you may be able to bear it.

1 CORINTHIANS 10:13

OCTOBER 24

*W*e can study all we want in His holy manual of life and learn everything we are supposed to do, but at some point we still have to jump in the water. The proof of our sincerity is in the *doing*, not just the knowing. Obedience is something you *do*; having a heart to obey is something you pray and ask God to give you.

MARCH 10

*L*ord, help me to be strong in my mind and spirit so I don't fall into any traps of the enemy. Do not allow me to be led into temptation, but deliver me from the evil one and his plans for my downfall.

OCTOBER 23

$\mathcal{L}$ord, Your Word says that those of us who love Your law will have great peace and nothing will cause us to stumble.

Great peace have those who love Your law, and nothing causes them to stumble.

PSALM 119:165

MARCH 11

$\mathcal{D}$on't let the devil rob you of all God has for you by tempting you with impure thoughts. If you ever find yourself with any kind of unholy attraction, confess it immediately before God and ask Him to set you free from it. Then tell Satan you recognize his plan to destroy you and separate you from all God has for you, and you are not going to allow him to do it.

Watch and pray, lest you enter into temptation. The spirit indeed is willing, but the flesh is weak.

MATTHEW 26:41

OCTOBER 22

We have no excuse for not doing what we need to do when God says He will *enable* us to do it if we will just call upon Him for help. All we have to say is, "Lord, help me to be disciplined enough to obey You the way You want me to so I can become the person You created me to be."

$\mathcal{B}$eloved, do not think it strange concerning the fiery trial which is to try you, as though some strange thing happened to you; but rejoice to the extent that you partake of Christ's sufferings, that when His glory is revealed, you may also be glad with exceeding joy.

1 PETER 4:12-13

OCTOBER 21

We know a lot about what we're *supposed* to be doing, but we often have a hard time *doing* it. We must pray that God will enable us to be disciplined enough to do what we need to do.

MARCH 13

*L*ord, I pray that You, O God of hope, will fill me with all joy and peace and faith so that I will "abound in hope by the power of the Holy Spirit" (Romans 15:13). Thank You that You have sent Your Holy Spirit to be my Comforter and Helper. Remind me of that in the midst of difficult times.

OCTOBER 20

*L*ord, I love Your law because I know it is good and it is there for my benefit. Enable me to live in obedience to each part of it so that I will not stumble and fall. Help me to obey You so that I can dwell in the confidence and peace of knowing I am living Your way.

He who has My commandments and keeps them, it is he who loves Me. And he who loves Me will be loved by My Father, and I will love him and manifest Myself to him.

JOHN 14:21

MARCH 14

$\mathcal{E}$very time you rise above the pain in your life and find the goodness, clarity, peace, and light of the Lord there, your faith will increase. God will meet you in the midst of your pain and not only perfect you, but increase your compassion for the sufferings of others. As you continue to live in the presence of the Lord, His glory will be revealed in you.

OCTOBER 19

*W*e must never get prideful about how perfectly we are obeying God because He is continually stretching us and asking us to move into new levels of growth. Without the perfecting, balancing, refining work of His Holy Spirit, the freedom you have in Christ will turn into a license to do anything you want.

MARCH 15

*W*hen we turn to the Holy Spirit for help and comfort, He will not only give us aid, but He will give us a richer portion of His presence than we have ever had before. We will be blessed when we mourn, because it will be the Comforter who comforts us (Matthew 5:4).

OCTOBER 18

*I*n addition to the rules we all have to obey, there are specific things God asks each of us to do as individuals in order to move us into the purpose He has for our lives. It's important that you keep asking God to show you what He wants *you* to do.

*L*ord, help me to remember to give thanks to You in all things, knowing that You reign in the midst of them. Remind me that You have redeemed me and I am Yours, and nothing is more important than that. I know when I pass through the waters You will be with me and the river will not overflow me. When I walk through the fire I will not be burned, nor will the flame touch me (Isaiah 43:1-2).

OCTOBER 17

$\mathcal{M}$y heart wants to obey You in all things, Lord. Show me where I am not doing that. If there are steps of obedience I need to take that I don't understand, I pray You would open my eyes to see the truth and help me to take those steps.

He who keeps His commandments abides in Him, and He in him. And by this we know that He abides in us, by the Spirit whom He has given us.

1 JOHN 3:24

MARCH 17

*S*ometimes difficult things happen to us so that the glory and power of God can be revealed in and through us. We may not be able to understand why certain things are happening at the time, and we may never know why we have to go through them until we go to be with the Lord, but when we turn to God in the midst of difficult situations, God's glory will be seen in them and on you.

OCTOBER 16

*W*e all have to do things we don't want to do. Part of being successful in life means doing things we would rather not. When we do things we don't like simply because we know we need to do them, it builds character in us. It makes us disciplined. It forms us into a leader God can trust.

If anyone loves Me, he will keep My word; and My Father will love him, and We will come to him and make Our home with him.

JOHN 14:23

MARCH 18

*L*ord, in times of grief, suffering, or trial, I pray for an added sense of Your presence. I want to grow stronger in these times and not weaker. I want to increase in faith and not be overcome with doubt. I want to have hope in the midst of it and not surrender to hopelessness. I want to stand strong in Your truth and not be swept away by my emotions.

*W*hen you find it difficult to do what you *know* you need to, ask the Holy Spirit to help you. Of course, you still have to take the first step, no matter how daunting, intimidating, dreadful, uncomfortable, or distasteful. But when you do, the Holy Spirit will assist you the rest of the way.

I will put My Spirit within you and cause you to walk in My statues, and you will keep My judgments and do them.

Ezekiel 36:27

MARCH 19

*T*ough times happen to everyone at one time or another. Pain and loss are a part of life. There are many different reasons why these things occur, but God is always there to bring good out of it when we invite Him to. If we understand the different possibilities for our suffering, it will help us overcome our pain and see our faith grow in the midst of it.

OCTOBER 14

*L*ord, I know I can't do all things right without Your help, so I ask that You would enable me to live in obedience to Your ways.

With my whole heart I have sought You; oh, let me not wander from Your commandments!

PSALM 119:10

MARCH 20

*O*nly You, Lord, can take whatever loss I experience and fill that empty place with good. Only You can take the burden of my grief and pain and dry my tears.

Hear me when I call, O God of my righteousness! You have relieved me in my distress; have mercy on me, and hear my prayer.

PSALM 4:1

OCTOBER 13

$\mathcal{G}$od has great plans for you. He has important things He wants you to do. And He is preparing you for your destiny right now. But you have to take steps of obedience in order to get there. And you have to trust that He knows the way and won't hurt you in the process.

MARCH 21

Just as we don't have to beg the sun for light, we don't have to beg the Holy Spirit for comfort either. He is comfort. We simply have to separate ourselves from anything that separates us from Him. We have to pray that when we go through difficult times, He will give us a greater sense of His comfort in it.

OCTOBER 12

$\mathcal{T}$here is a direct connection between obedience and getting your prayers answered. Don't keep telling God what *you* want without asking Him what *He* wants.

And whatever we ask we receive from Him, because we keep His commandments and do those things that are pleasing in His sight.

1 JOHN 3:22

MARCH 22

*L*ord, help me to remember that no matter how dark my situation may become, You are the light of my life and can never be put out. No matter what dark clouds settle on my life, you will lift me above the storm and into the comfort of Your presence.

But may the God of all grace, who called us to His eternal glory by Christ Jesus, after you have suffered a while, perfect, establish, strengthen, and settle you.

1 PETER 5:10

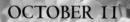

OCTOBER 11

*Y*ou never know when you will step into the moment for which God has been preparing you. And it is not just one moment; it's many successive ones. It doesn't matter whether you are a single career woman or a married lady with nine children under the age of ten, it doesn't matter whether you are nineteen or ninety, God is preparing you daily for something great.

MARCH 23

*W*hen the dark clouds of trial, struggle, grief, or suffering roll in and settle on us so thick that we can barely see ahead of us, it's easy to forget there is a place of calm, light, clarity, and peace we can rise to. If we take God's hand in those difficult times, He will lift us up above our circumstances to the place of comfort, warmth, and safety He has for us.

OCTOBER 10

*G*od wants you to be willing to let Him purify you, fortify you, and grow you up in Him. But you have to play by the rules.

If anyone competes in athletics, he is not crowned unless he competes according to the rules.

2 TIMOTHY 2:5

MARCH 24

Come to Me, all you who labor and are heavy laden, and I will give you rest. Take My yoke upon you and learn from Me, for I am gentle and lowly in heart, and you will find rest for your souls. For My yoke is easy and My burden is light.

MATTHEW 11:28-30

OCTOBER 9

*L*ord, reveal to me when I am *not* doing things I should be doing. Show me if I am doing things I should not. Help me to hear Your specific instructions to me. Speak to me clearly through Your Word. Help me to be ever learning about Your ways so I can live in the fullness of Your presence and move into all You have for me.

For the Lord God is a sun and shield; the Lord will give grace and glory; no good thing will He withhold from those who walk uprightly.

PSALM 84:11

MARCH 25

$\mathcal{T}$hank You, Lord, that in my distress I can call on You. And when I cry out to You, Lord, You hear my voice and answer (Psalm 18:6). May the joy of knowing You fill my heart with happiness and peace.

OCTOBER 8

*W*e all have an enemy who is like a terrorist to our soul. If we don't realize this, it will be easy for him to manipulate us. Of course, he is not omniscient nor omnipresent—he can't be everywhere and know our every thought—but if we don't fully realize that he is a limited and defeated foe, then we will be harassed by him continually.

MARCH 26

*N*egative emotions reveal doubt. If we thoroughly trust God, what do we have to be anxious about? Yet we all are susceptible to experiencing these kinds of emotions at some time in our life. Don't feel bad about having them, but don't live with them either. Refuse to allow the ugliness of negative emotions to mar the beauty of the life God has for you.

OCTOBER 7

One of the things Jesus accomplished when He died and rose again was to break the power of the enemy. When He defeated the enemy on the cross, He gave us authority over him. He said, "I give you the authority…over all the power of the enemy, and nothing shall by any means hurt you" (Luke 10:19).

MARCH 27

*N*o matter how bad things appear to get in your life, you *always* have hope in the Lord. Ask God to give you hope for your future and an attitude of gratefulness every day of your life.

Those who wait on the Lord shall renew their strength; they shall mount up with wings like eagles, they shall run and not be weary, they shall walk and not faint.

ISAIAH 40:31

OCTOBER 6

*L*ord, I thank You for suffering and dying on the cross for me, and for rising again to defeat death and hell. My enemy is defeated because of what You have done. Thank You that You have given me all authority over him.

Behold, I give you the authority to trample on serpents and scorpions, and over all the power of the enemy, and nothing shall by any means hurt you.

LUKE 10:19

MARCH 28

When a root of bitterness takes hold of your life, it consumes you and cuts off the blessings of God. Pray for God to set you free from any bitterness. Ask Him to give you a spirit of thankfulness, praise, and worship. Ask the Holy Spirit to crowd out anything in your heart that is not of Him.

OCTOBER 5

Finally, my brethren, be strong in the Lord and in the power of His might. Put on the whole armor of God, that you may be able to stand against the wiles of the devil.

EPHESIANS 6:10-11

MARCH 29

So many of us live with depression and accept it without even realizing it. The good news is that God doesn't want us to live with these feelings. He wants us to have the joy of the Lord rise in us and chase away spirits of heaviness. God wants us to cry out to Him so He can lift us out of depression.

Depart from me, all you workers of iniquity; for the Lord has heard the voice of my weeping. The Lord has heard my supplication; the Lord will receive my prayer.

PSALM 6:8-9

OCTOBER 4

*L*ord, by the power of Your Holy Spirit I can successfully resist the devil and he must flee from me. Show me when I am not recognizing the encroachment of the enemy in my life. Teach me to use that authority You have given me to see him defeated in every area.

Therefore submit to God. Resist the devil and he will flee from you.

JAMES 4:7

MARCH 30

*L*ord, help me to not be insecure and self-focused so that I miss opportunities to focus on You and extend Your love. May I be sensitive to the needs, trials, and weaknesses of others and not oversensitive to myself. What You accomplished on the cross is my source of greatest joy. Help me to concentrate on that.

OCTOBER 3

$\mathcal{T}$his is the deal. The devil has come to steal, kill, and destroy. Jesus has come to give you life abundantly. Ask God to show you the truth about your situation. Don't let the enemy of your soul talk you into accepting anything less than what God has for you.

MARCH 31

*W*hen we have constant unrest because we are never at peace, it not only makes *us* miserable—it makes everyone around us miserable too. "There remains therefore a rest for the people of God" (Hebrews 4:9). It's possible to find contentment, rest, peace, and joy in any situation. Tell God you are making that your goal and you need Him to help you.

OCTOBER 2

*L*ord, reveal to me any place in my life where I am walking in disobedience. If I have given the enemy a place in my protective armor through which he can secure a hook, show me so I can rectify it. Gird me with strong faith in You and in Your Word. Thank You that I will never be brought down by the enemy as long as I stand strong in You.

But the Lord is faithful, who will establish you and guard you from the evil one.

2 THESSALONIANS 3:3

APRIL 1

Only foolish people are quick to get angry. People with wisdom don't want to pay the price. "Do not hasten in your spirit to be angry, for anger rests in the bosom of fools" (Ecclesiastes 7:9). Ask God to keep you free from anger so you can remain in the flow of all God has for you.

OCTOBER I

$\mathcal{T}$herefore take up the whole armor of God, that you may be able to withstand in the evil day, and having done all, to stand. Stand therefore, having girded your waist with truth, having put on the breastplate of righteousness, and having shod your feet with the preparation of the gospel of peace; above all, taking the shield of faith with which you will be able to quench all the fiery darts of the wicked one. And take the helmet of salvation, and the sword of the Spirit, which is the word of God.

EPHESIANS 6:13-17

APRIL 2

$\mathcal{B}$e anxious for nothing, but in everything by prayer and supplication, with thanksgiving, let your requests be made known to God; and the peace of God, which surpasses all understanding, will guard your hearts and minds through Christ Jesus.

PHILIPPIANS 4:6-7

SEPTEMBER 30

A big part of standing against the enemy of our souls is taking control over our minds. As the Bible says, we must learn to bring every thought into captivity.

Casting down arguments and every high thing that exalts itself against the knowledge of God, bringing every thought into captivity to the obedience of Christ.

2 CORINTHIANS 10:5

APRIL 3

When you are anxious, it means you aren't trusting God to take care of you. But He will prove His faithfulness if you run to Him.

Do not seek what you should eat or what you should drink, nor have an anxious mind. For all these things the nations of the world seek after, and your Father knows that you need these things. But seek the kingdom of God, and all these things shall be added to you.

Luke 12:29-31

SEPTEMBER 29

*L*ord, help me to never exchange Your truth for a lie. Where I have accepted a lie as truth, reveal that to me. Help me to clearly discern when it is the enemy who is speaking.

APRIL 4

$\mathcal{L}$ord, help me to live in Your joy and peace. Give me strength and understanding to resist anxiety, anger, unrest, envy, depressions, bitterness, hopelessness, loneliness, fear, and guilt. Rescue me when "my spirit is overwhelmed within me; my heart within me is distressed" (Psalm 143:4).

SEPTEMBER 28

*L*ife has much suffering, but too often we suffer unnecessarily because of lies we believe about ourselves and our circumstances. We accept as fact the words that are spoken to our souls by an enemy who wants us destroyed. But we can overcome each one of these lies with prayer, faith, and the truth of God's Word.

APRIL 5

We all have difficult times. Times when we feel all alone and abandoned. But the truth is we aren't. God is with us to help us when we call upon Him. In the midst of these times, we don't have to be controlled by our negative emotions. We can resist them by praying and knowing the truth of what God's Word says about them.

The righteous cry out, and the Lord hears, and delivers them out of all their troubles. The Lord is near to those who have a broken heart, and saves such as have a contrite spirit.

Psalm 34:17-18

SEPTEMBER 27

$\mathcal{A}$nd do not be conformed to this world, but be transformed by the renewing of your mind, that you may prove what is that good and acceptable and perfect will of God.

ROMANS 12:2

APRIL 6

*H*ave you ever felt as though God has forsaken you? Well, if you have, you're not alone. In fact, you are in very good company. Not only do millions of other people feel that way right now, but Jesus felt that way at one time too. At the lowest point in His life, Jesus said, "My God my God, why have You forsaken Me?" (Matthew 27:46).

*Y*ou don't have to live with confusion or mental oppression. Instead you can have clarity and knowledge. Even though your enemy tries to convince you that your future is as hopeless as his, or that you are a failure with no purpose, value, gifts, or abilities, God says exactly the opposite. Believe God and don't listen to anything else.

APRIL 7

I will give you the keys of the kingdom of heaven, and whatever you bind on earth will be bound in heaven, and whatever you loose on earth will be loosed in heaven.

MATTHEW 16:19

SEPTEMBER 25

*T*hank You, Lord, that I "have the mind of Christ" (1 Corinthians 2:16). I want Your thoughts to be my thoughts. Show me where I have filled my mind with anything that is ungodly.

APRIL 8

*I*n Jesus' name, I pray that every stronghold erected around me by the enemy will be brought down to nothing. I know that You who have begun a good work in me will complete it (Philippians 1:6). Give me patience to not give up and the strength to stand strong in Your Word.

SEPTEMBER 24

$\mathcal{F}$or though we walk in the flesh, we do not war according to the flesh. For the weapons of our warfare are not carnal but mighty in God for pulling down strongholds, casting down arguments and every high thing that exalts itself against the knowledge of God, bringing every thought into captivity to the obedience of Christ.

2 CORINTHIANS 10:3-5

APRIL 9

*G*od will not rest until your righteousness goes forth as brightness and your salvation as a lamp that burns (Isaiah 62:1). Deliverance won't change you into someone else. It will release you to be who you really are—an intelligent, secure, loving, talented, kindhearted, witty, attractive, wonderful woman of God.

SEPTEMBER 23

*L*ord, help me to think upon what is true, noble, just, pure, lovely, of good report, virtuous, and praiseworthy (Philippians 4:8). I lay claim to the "sound mind" that You have given me.

For God has not given us a spirit of fear, but of power and of love and of a sound mind.

2 TIMOTHY 1:7

APRIL 10

*G*od does a complete work, and He will see it through to the end. So don't give up because it's taking longer than you hoped. Be confident that "He who has begun a good work in you will complete it until the day of Jesus Christ" (Philippians 1:6).

SEPTEMBER 22

*S*urrendering everything means being willing to say, "Lord, whatever You want me to do I'll do it. I say yes to anything You ask of me, even if it means dying to myself and my desires. I will give up the things of the flesh that I want in order to have more of You in my life." This attitude of surrender means putting God first and submitting to His rulership. And it makes all the difference in our lives.

APRIL 11

*R*emember that deliverance comes from the Lord, and it is an ongoing process. It is God who has "delivered us from so great a death, and does deliver us; in whom we trust that He will still deliver us" (2 Corinthians 1:10).

SEPTEMBER 21

Lord, I bow before You this day and declare that You are Lord over every area of my life. I surrender myself and my life to You and invite You to rule in every part of my mind, soul, body, and spirit.

APRIL 12

I call upon You, Lord, and ask that You would deliver me from anything that binds me or separates me from You. Where I have opened the door for the enemy with my own desires, I repent of that. Where I am walking in disobedience, show me so I can turn and live in obedience to Your ways. Give me wisdom to walk the right way and strength to rise above the things that would pull me down (Proverbs 28:26).

SEPTEMBER 20

$\mathcal{T}$rust in the Lord with all your heart, and lean not on your own understanding; in all your ways acknowledge Him, and He shall direct your paths.

PROVERBS 3:5-6

APRIL 13

*E*very time you worship God something happens in the spirit realm to break the power of evil. That's because He inhabits your praises, and this means you are in His presence. "Now the Lord is the Spirit; and where the Spirit of the Lord is, there is liberty" (2 Corinthians 3:17).

SEPTEMBER 19

*L*ord, I love You with all my heart, with all my soul, and with all my mind. I commit to trusting You with my whole being. I declare You to be Lord over every area of my life today and every day.

*N*o matter how strong the thing is you're struggling with, God's power to deliver you is stronger.

For He looked down from the height of His sanctuary, from heaven the Lord viewed the earth, to hear the groaning of the prisoner, to release those appointed to death.

PSALM 102:19-20

SEPTEMBER 18

*G*od is not only Lord over the universe, He is Lord over our individual lives as well. Whether we acknowledge that or not will determine the success and quality of our life. If we would drop everything and say, "I give up, Lord. I surrender. Take everything. I will do whatever You say," our lives would be better in every way.

Without You, Lord, I am held captive by my desires, I am blind to the truth, and I am oppressed. But with You comes freedom from all that.

My times are in Your hand; deliver me from the hand of my enemies, and from those who persecute me.

PSALM 31:15

SEPTEMBER 17

$\mathcal{L}$ord, enable me to deny myself in order to take up my cross daily and follow you (Luke 9:23). I want to be Your disciple just as You have said in Your Word.

And whoever does not bear his cross and come after Me cannot be My disciple.

LUKE 14:27

APRIL 16

*J*esus came to set us free from all the things that bind us. He came to lift us above the enemy who wants to destroy us. God hears the groaning of those who are held captive. If you cry out to Him, He will set you free. And "if the Son makes you free, you shall be free indeed" (John 8:36).

SEPTEMBER 16

*J*esus said, "Whoever does not bear his cross and come after Me cannot be My disciple" (Luke 14:27). You can't bear His cross unless you surrender Your life to Him. A surrendered life, a life ruled entirely by God, is one that can be used powerfully for His kingdom purposes.

APRIL 17

*L*ord, I know that I can't see all the ways the enemy wants to erect strongholds in my life. I depend on You to reveal them to me. Thank You that You came to "proclaim liberty to the captives and recovery of sight to the blind, to set at liberty those who are oppressed" (Luke 4:18).

SEPTEMBER 15

$\mathcal{L}$ord, help me to do what it takes. I want to lose my life in You so I can save it. Teach me what that means. Speak to me so that I may understand.

For whoever desires to save his life will lose it, but whoever loses his life for My sake will save it.

LUKE 9:24

APRIL 18

*W*e all need deliverance at one time or another. That's because no matter how spiritual we are, we're still made of flesh. And no matter how perfectly we live, we still have an enemy who is trying to erect strongholds of evil in our lives. God wants us free from everything that binds, holds, or separates us from Him.

Because he has set his love upon Me, therefore I will deliver him; I will set him on high, because he has known My name.

PSALM 91:14

God doesn't want just part of you. He wants it all. Pray that you will give God what He wants.

APRIL 19

If you cry out for discernment, and lift up your voice for understanding, if you seek her as silver, and search for her as for hidden treasures; then you will understand the fear of the Lord, and find the knowledge of God. For the Lord gives wisdom; from His mouth come knowledge and understanding.

PROVERBS 2:3-6

SEPTEMBER 13

*L*ord, help me to say yes to You immediately when You give me direction for my life. My desire is to please You and hold nothing back.

I don't want to trust my own heart, Lord. I want to trust Your Word and Your instruction so that I will walk wisely and never do ignorant or stupid things. Make me to be a wise person.

As you have therefore received Christ Jesus the Lord, so walk in Him, rooted and built up in Him and established in the faith, as you have been taught, abounding in it with thanksgiving.

COLOSSIANS 2:6-7

APRIL 21

$\mathcal{W}$e have no idea how many times simple wisdom has saved our lives or kept us out of harm's way or how many times it will be so in the future. That's why we can't live without it and need to ask God for it. We have to pray, "Lord give me wisdom in all I do. Help me to walk in wisdom every day."

SEPTEMBER 11

*L*ord, I declare this day that "I have been crucified with Christ; it is no longer I who live, but Christ lives in me; and the life which I now live in the flesh I live by faith in the Son of God, who loved me and gave Himself for me" (Galatians 2:20). Rule me in every area of my life, Lord, and lead me into all that You have for me.

APRIL 22

*T*he mouth of the righteous speaks wisdom, and his tongue talks of justice. The law of his God is in his heart; none of his steps shall slide.

PSALM 37:30-31

SEPTEMBER 10

*L*ord, I surrender my relationships, my finances, my work, my recreation, my decisions, my time, my body, my mind, my soul, my desires, and my dreams. I put them all in Your hands so they can be used for Your glory.

Therefore humble yourselves under the mighty hand of God, that He may exalt you in due time, casting all your cares upon Him, for He cares for you.

1 PETER 5:6-7

APRIL 23

*L*ord, help me to always seek godly counsel and not look to the world and ungodly people for answers. Thank You, Lord, that You will give me the counsel and instruction I need. Thank You that "You will show me the path of life" (Psalm 16:11).

SEPTEMBER 9

Shouldn't we pray *every* time we read the Bible, "Lord, take me deeper into Your Word"? Our time in God's Word is one of the most important aspects of our lives, and it should be covered in prayer.

*T*hank You, Lord, that You give "wisdom to the wise and knowledge to those who have understanding" (Daniel 2:21). Increase my wisdom and knowledge so I can see Your truth in every situation. Give me discernment for each decision I must make.

SEPTEMBER 8

$\mathcal{L}$ord, I thank You for Your Word. "Your Word is a lamp to my feet and a light to my path" (Psalm 119:105). It is food to my soul, and I can't live without it. Enable me to truly comprehend its deepest meaning.

APRIL 25

$\mathcal{T}$he fear of the Lord is the beginning of wisdom, and the knowledge of the Holy One is understanding. For by me your days will be multiplied, and years of life will be added to you.

PROVERBS 9:10-11

God's Word is food for our souls. We can't live without it. It is written that "man shall not live by bread alone, but by every word that proceeds from the mouth of God" (Matthew 4:4). If we are not continually fed with God's Word, we will starve spiritually.

APRIL 26

*W*isdom means making the right choice or decision. And only God knows what that is.

However, when He, the Spirit of truth, has come, He will guide you into all truth; for He will not speak on His own authority, but whatever He hears He will speak; and He will tell you things to come.

JOHN 16:13

SEPTEMBER 6

*L*ord, give me greater understanding than I have ever had before, and reveal to me the hidden treasures buried in Your Word. I pray that I will have a heart that is teachable and open to what You want me to know. I desire Your instruction. Teach me so I may learn.

APRIL 27

*W*isdom means having clear understanding and insight.
It means knowing how to apply the truth in every situation.
It's discerning what is right and wrong. It's having good
judgment. It's being able to sense when you are getting
too close to the edge.

SEPTEMBER 5

*F*or the word of God is living and powerful, and sharper than any two-edged sword, piercing even to the division of soul and spirit, and of joints and marrow, and is a discerner of the thoughts and intents of the heart.

HEBREWS 4:12

APRIL 28

*L*ord, I pray You would give me Your wisdom and understanding in all things. I know wisdom is better than gold and understanding better than silver (Proverbs 16:16), so make me rich in wisdom and wealthy in understanding.

SEPTEMBER 4

*H*elp me, Lord, to be diligent to put Your Word inside my soul faithfully every day. Show me where I'm wasting time that could be better spent reading Your Word. Give me the ability to memorize it. Etch it in my mind and heart. Make it become a part of me. Change me as I read it.

APRIL 29

$\mathcal{S}$ometimes we are very close to the edge of a dangerous situation. But God sees it all because He is above all. If we were to connect with Him on a regular basis and say, "Lord, guide me so I won't fall," He could lead us away from the edge.

SEPTEMBER 3

*I*t is important for each of us to *guard* the Word of God that has been deposited in our souls. "Therefore we must give the more earnest heed to the things we have heard, lest we drift away" (Hebrews 2:1).

$\mathcal{T}$hank You, Lord, that "I will both lie down in peace, and sleep; for You alone, O Lord, make me dwell in safety" (Psalm 4:8). Thank You for Your promises of protection. I lay claim to them this day.

SEPTEMBER 2

It doesn't matter how long you walk with God; He always has new things for you to learn. It may be new dimensions of what you already know, or it may be something you have never seen before. Either way, it's not enough to just *learn* the truth; you must *act* on it.

MAY 1

*H*e shall cover you with His feathers, and under His wings you shall take refuge; His truth shall be your shield and buckler. You shall not be afraid of the terror by night, nor of the arrow that flies by day, nor of the pestilence that walks in darkness, nor of the destruction that lays waste at noonday. A thousand may fall at your side, and ten thousand at your right hand; but it shall not come near you.

PSALM 91:4-7

SEPTEMBER 1

*B*lessed is the man who walks not in the counsel of the ungodly, nor stands in the path of sinners, nor sits in the seat of the scornful; but his delight is in the law of the Lord, and in His law he meditates day and night. He shall be like a tree planted by the rivers of water, that brings forth its fruit in its season, whose leaf also shall not wither; and whatever he does shall prosper.

PSALM 1:1-3

MAY 2

*Y*ou, Lord, are my refuge and strength and "a very present help in trouble." Therefore I will not fear, "even though the earth be removed and though the mountains be carried into the midst of the sea" (Psalm 46:1-2).

AUGUST 31

*L*ord, I don't want to be just a hearer of Your Word. Show me how to be a doer of Your Word as well. Enable me to respond the way I should and obey You. Show me when I am not doing what it says. Help me to apply my heart to Your instruction and my ears to Your Words of knowledge (Proverbs 23:12).

MAY 3

*L*ord, I want to dwell in Your secret place and abide in Your shadow. Keep me under the umbrella of Your protection. Help me never to stray from the center of Your will or off the path You have for me. Enable me to always hear Your voice guiding me.

He who dwells in the secret place of the Most High shall abide under the shadow of the Almighty.

PSALM 91:1

AUGUST 30

*W*henever you read God's Word, it is essential to ask Him to help you practically apply it to your life. Take a step that indicates you believe what you read and are going to live like it.

MAY 4

*W*hen you pass through the waters, I will be with you; and through the rivers, they shall not overflow you. When you walk through the fire, you shall not be burned, nor shall the flame scorch you.

ISAIAH 43:2

AUGUST 29

*G*od has gold nuggets and diamonds everywhere in His Word, but we must dig them out. And, just like precious gems and metals when they are first pulled from the ground, the treasures of God's Word need to be polished and refined in us in order to have the brilliance they are capable of revealing.

MAY 5

*L*ord, I trust in Your Word, which assures me that You are my rock, my fortress, my deliverer, my shield, my stronghold, and my strength in whom I trust.

Because you have made the Lord, who is my refuge, even the Most High, your dwelling place, no evil shall befall you, nor shall any plague come near your dwelling.

PSALM 91:9-10

AUGUST 28

$\mathcal{E}$very time you go over one of God's promises in your heart, it will become more refined and polished in you and shine more brightly in your soul.

But he who looks into the perfect law of liberty and continues in it, and is not a forgetful hearer but a doer of the work, this one will be blessed in what he does.

JAMES 1:25

MAY 6

$\mathcal{G}$od is a place of safety you can run to, but it helps if you are running to Him on a daily basis so that you are in familiar territory. The Bible says, "In the fear of the Lord there is strong confidence, and His children will have a place of refuge. The fear of the Lord is a fountain of life, to turn one away from the snares of death" (Proverbs 14:26-27).

AUGUST 27

*T*hank You, Lord, that when I look into Your Word I find You. Help me to know You better through it. Give me ears to recognize Your voice speaking to me every time I read it. I don't want to ever miss the way You are leading me.

*L*ord, I pray for Your hand of protection to be upon me. Keep me safe from any accidents, diseases, or evil influences. Protect me wherever I go. Keep me safe in planes, cars, or any other means of transportation.

One of the most priceless gems you will find in God's Word is His voice. That's because He speaks to us through His Word as we read it or hear it. In fact, we can't really learn to recognize God's voice whispering to our soul if we are not first hearing Him speak to us in His Word.

MAY 8

*O*ur heavenly Father looks out for us and protects us from danger far more than we realize. But it's not something we can take for granted. It's something we must pray about often.

AUGUST 25

$\mathcal{T}$he Word straightens out our mind and soul and helps us think clearly about things. It leads us away from self-destructive thoughts and enables us to enjoy a sense of well-being. It gives us hope and keeps us on course. It provides us a solid foundation upon which to build a life of wholeness. Ask God to meet you in His Word every day. He looks forward to that, and He wants you to also.

MAY 9

$\mathcal{L}$ord, I pray *You* would direct my steps. Only You know the way I should go. I don't want to get off the path You want me to walk on and end up in the wrong place. I want to move into all You have for me and become all You made me to be by walking in Your perfect will for my life now.

For you have need of endurance, so that after you have done the will of God, you may receive the promise.

HEBREWS 10:36

AUGUST 24

*T*here is no way to draw closer to God, or have a clean and right heart before Him, or be a forgiving person, or walk in obedience to His ways, or take control of your mind, or stand against the enemy, or make Jesus Lord of your life unless you are in the Word of God every day. It's your compass. Your guide. You can't get where you need to go without it.

MAY 10

God gave us a choice as to whether we subject our will to Him or not. We make that decision every day. Will we *seek* His will? Will we *ask* Him for wisdom? Will we *do* what He says? God's will is the way we choose to live each day of our lives.

Therefore do not be unwise, but understand what the will of the Lord is.

EPHESIANS 5:17

AUGUST 23

*L*ord, when I hear Your voice and follow You, my life is full. When I get off the path You have for me, my life is empty. Guide, perfect, and fill me with Your Word this day.

MAY 11

*L*ord, align my heart with Yours. Help me to hear Your voice saying, "This is the way, walk in it." If I am doing anything outside of Your will, show me. Speak to me from Your Word so that I will have understanding. If there is something I should be doing, reveal it to me so that I can correct my course. I want to do only what You want me to do.

AUGUST 22

*W*hoever keeps His word, truly the love of God is perfected in him. By this we know that we are in Him.

1 JOHN 2:5

MAY 12

Don't think that trouble in your life means you are out of God's will. God uses the trouble you have to perfect you. There is a big difference between being out of God's will and being pruned or tested by God. Both are uncomfortable, but one leads to life and one doesn't. In one you will have peace, no matter how uncomfortable it gets. In the other, you won't.

AUGUST 21

*W*e can't live successfully without right priorities in our lives. Correct priorities are not something we can figure out on our own. We have to be led by the Holy Spirit and have a clear knowledge of God's Word in order to understand what they should be.

MAY 13

*G*uide my every step, Lord. Lead me "in Your righteousness" and "make Your way straight before my face" (Psalm 5:8). As I draw close and walk in intimate relationship with You each day, I pray You will get me where I need to go.

Our two most important priorities come directly from the Word of God. Jesus told us about them, saying, "'You shall love the Lord your God with all your heart, with all your soul, and with all your mind.' This is the first and great commandment. And the second is like it: 'You shall love your neighbor as yourself'" (Matthew 22:37-39).

MAY 14

*T*rouble is a part of life. Having fulfillment and peace in the midst of trouble is what living in God's will is all about. There is great confidence in knowing that you are walking in the will of God and doing what He wants you to do. When you are sure of that, you can better deal with what life brings you.

*L*ord, I pray You would help me set my life in right order. I want to always put You first above all else in my life. Teach me how to love You with all my heart, mind, and soul.

MAY 15

$\mathcal{L}$ord, I pray You will fill me with the "knowledge of [Your] will in all wisdom and spiritual understanding" (Colossians 1:9). Help me to walk in a worthy manner, fully pleasing to You, being fruitful in every good work and increasing in the knowledge of Your ways.

AUGUST 18

*Y*our relationship with the Lord must always have top priority over everything else. The Lord said, "You shall have no other gods before Me" (Exodus 20:3), and He means it. God wants your *undivided* attention.

MAY 16

God's will is a place of safety. When we walk in the will of God, we find safety. When we live outside of God's will, we forfeit His protection. We must regularly ask God to show us what His will is and lead us in it. We must ask Him to speak to our heart so He can tell us.

Your ears shall hear a word behind you, saying, "This is the way, walk in it," whenever you turn to the right hand or whenever you turn to the left.

ISAIAH 30:21

AUGUST 17

God is a God of order. We can tell that by looking at the universe. None of it is random or accidental. He doesn't want our lives to be either. His will is that we "let all things be done decently and in order" (I Corinthians 14:40). And when we pray to Him about it, He will help us do just that.

MAY 17

*W*e should no longer be children, tossed to and fro and carried about with every wind of doctrine, by the trickery of men, in the cunning craftiness of deceitful plotting, but, speaking the truth in love, may grow up in all things into Him who is the head—Christ—from whom the whole body, joined and knit together by what every joint supplies, according to the effective working by which every part does its share, causes growth of the body for the edifying of itself in love.

EPHESIANS 4:14-16

AUGUST 16

*L*ord, I don't want to have any other gods but You in my life. Show me if I have lifted up my soul to an idol. My desire is to serve You and only You. Help me to live accordingly.

MAY 18

*L*ord, I pray for godly friends, role models, and mentors to come into my life. Send people who will speak the truth in love. I pray especially that there will be women in my life who are trustworthy, kind, loving, and faithful. Most of all I pray that they be women of strong faith who will add to my life and I to theirs.

AUGUST 15

*G*od will show us how to align ourselves under proper authority so that we can come under the covering of His protection. This is crucial to our moving into all God has for us.

Godly people will help you walk in the right direction, and the good in them will rub off on you. The quality of your relationships will determine the quality of your life. And this is something worth praying about.

AUGUST 14

Submission is something you *decide* to do, not something someone *forces* you to do. The meaning of the word "submit" is "to submit yourself." It's a condition of the heart. Having a submitted heart means you are *willing* to submit yourself and come into proper alignment in accordance with God's will.

*T*hroughout your whole life relationships will be crucial to your well-being. It is not emotionally or spiritually healthy to be isolated. Right relationships will enrich and balance you and give you a healthy perspective.

AUGUST 13

*G*ive me a submissive heart, Lord. Help me to always submit to the governing authorities and the correct people in my family, work, and church. Show me who the proper spiritual authorities are to be in my life.

All of you be submissive to one another, and be clothed with humility, for "God resists the proud, but gives grace to the humble."

1 PETER 5:5

MAY 21

*D*on't leave your relationships to chance. Pray for godly people to come into your life with whom you can connect. Don't *force* relationships to happen, *pray* for them to happen. Then when they do, nurture them with prayer.

*J*esus Himself was submitted to God. His priorities were definitely in order. God desires that "this mind be in you which was also in Christ Jesus, who, being in the form of God, did not consider it robbery to be equal with God, but made Himself of no reputation, taking the form of a bondservant, and coming in the likeness of men. And being found in appearance as a man, He humbled Himself and became obedient to the point of death, even the death of the cross" (Philippians 2:5-8).

MAY 22

*L*et all bitterness, wrath, anger, clamor, and evil speaking be put away from you, with all malice. And be kind to one another, tenderhearted, forgiving one another, just as God in Christ forgave you.

EPHESIANS 4:31-32

AUGUST 11

$\mathcal{L}$ord, I know that if my life is not in proper order I will not receive the blessings You have for me. But I also know that if I seek You first, all that I need will be added to me.

Seek first the kingdom of God and His righteousness, and all these things shall be added to you.

MATTHEW 6:33

MAY 23

I pray, Lord, for my relationships with each of my family members. Specifically, I pray for my relationship with (name the family member for whom you are most concerned). I pray You would bring healing, reconciliation, and restoration where it is needed. Bless our relationship and make it strong.

*A*sk God to help you discern exactly to whom you are to be submitted and in what way. Don't just submit blindly or ignorantly. Know what you are doing. When your heart's desire is to do what's right and be in right order, God will help you find that perfect balance.

MAY 24

$\mathcal{A}$sk God to make you a good friend to others and give you a pure and loving heart in all your relationships. Pray especially for the people you live with. The Bible says that "every...house divided against itself will not stand" (Matthew 12:25). You can't have peace if you are living in discord with anyone in your home.

AUGUST 9

*S*ubmission to others takes a heart that loves others as ourselves. That's the key. When you love God first and others second, all the other priorities in your life will fall into place and you will be in right order. When you ask God to show you clearly what your priorities should be, He will.

MAY 25

*Y*ou are no longer strangers and foreigners, but fellow citizens with the saints and members of the household of God, having been built on the foundation of the apostles and prophets, Jesus Christ Himself being the chief corner stone, in whom the whole building, being joined together, grows into a holy temple in the Lord, in whom you also are being built together for a dwelling place of God in the Spirit.

EPHESIANS 2:19-22

AUGUST 8

*L*ord, I seek You first this day and ask that You would enable me to put my life in perfect order. May I never come out from under the covering of spiritual protection You have placed in my life.

MAY 26

*I*f it's true that we become like the friends we spend time with, then we must select our friends wisely. The person who will do what it takes to live in the perfect will of God is the kind of friend who imparts something of the goodness of the Lord to you every time you are with them.

*O*bey those who rule over you, and be submissive, for they watch out for your souls, as those who must give account. Let them do so with joy and not with grief, for that would be unprofitable for you.

HEBREWS 13:17

MAY 27

Lord, I lift up every one of my relationships to You and ask You to bless them. I pray that each one would be glorifying to You. Help me to choose my friends wisely so I won't be led astray. Give me discernment and strength to separate myself from anyone who is not a good influence. I release all my relationships to You and pray that Your will be done in each one of them.

AUGUST 6

$\mathcal{W}$hen we praise and worship God, it is like being hooked up to a spiritual IV. As long as we have our hearts and eyes lifted to God in worship and praise, the joy of the Lord can pour into our bodies, minds, souls, and spirits and crowd out any darkness and depression. Confusion, oppression, fear, or anxiety can't exist in the heart of a worshiping child of God.

MAY 28

*I*t's important to be yoked with people who walk closely with God. Accountability results from having close relationships with strong believers who are themselves accountable to other strong believers. It's important to be accountable because we are all capable of being deceived. We need people who will help us see the truth about ourselves and our lives.

$\mathcal{N}$othing we do is more powerful or more life-changing than praising God. It is one of the means by which God transforms us. Every time we praise and worship Him, His presence comes to dwell in us and changes our hearts and allows the Holy Spirit to soften and mold them into whatever He wants them to be.

MAY 29

We all desperately need a sense of family, of relationship, of belonging. God created us to be in families. We have a natural hunger to be a part of something that gives us a sense of acceptance, affirmation, and being needed and appreciated.

AUGUST 4

*L*ord, there is no source of greater joy for me than worshiping You. I come into Your presence with thanksgiving and bow before You this day. I exalt Your name, for You are great and worthy to be praised.

MAY 30

*I*n Him also we have obtained an inheritance, being predestined according to the purpose of Him who works all things according to the counsel of His will, that we who first trusted in Christ should be to the praise of His glory.

EPHESIANS 1:11-12

AUGUST 3

*B*ut the hour is coming, and now is, when the true worshipers will worship the Father in spirit and truth; for the Father is seeking such to worship Him. God is Spirit, and those who worship Him must worship in spirit and truth.

JOHN 4:23-24

MAY 31

$\mathcal{L}$ord, I pray that You would show me clearly what the gifts and talents are that You have placed in me. Lead me in the way I should go as I grow in them. Enable me to use them according to Your will and for Your glory.

$\mathscr{B}$ecause praise and worship is not something our flesh naturally *wants* to do, we have to *will* ourselves to do it. And because it's not the first thing we think of to do, we have to decide to do it no matter what our circumstances.

Keep in mind that God "has saved us and called us with a holy calling, not according to our works, but according to His own purpose and grace which was given to us in Christ Jesus before time began" (2 Timothy 1:9). May you never forget, dear sister, that God has an important purpose for your life and that it is good.

AUGUST 1

$\mathcal{T}$hank You, Lord, that "You have put gladness in my heart" (Psalm 4:7). All honor and majesty, strength and glory, holiness and righteousness are Yours, O Lord.

JUNE 2

We all need to have a sense of why we are here. We all need to know we were created for a purpose. We will never find fulfillment and happiness until we are doing the thing for which we were created. But God won't move us into the big things He has called us to unless we have been proven faithful in the small things He has given us.

*W*e can claim to know and love God, but if we are not worshiping and praising Him every day, we are in the dark about who He really is.

Although they knew God, they did not glorify Him as God, nor were thankful, but became futile in their thoughts, and their foolish hearts were darkened.

ROMANS 1:21

JUNE 3

I pray, Lord, that nothing will draw me away from fulfilling the plan You have for me. May I never stray from what You have called me to be and do. Give me a vision for my life and a strong sense of purpose. I put my identity in You and my destiny in Your hands.

JULY 30

Let all those rejoice who put their trust in You; let them ever shout for joy, because You defend them; let those also who love Your name be joyful in You. For You, O Lord, will bless the righteous; with favor You will surround him as with a shield.

PSALM 5:11-12

JUNE 4

*W*e can never move into all God has for us and become all He created us to be without surrendering our dreams to Him. Jesus said, "Whoever desires to save his life will lose it, but whoever loses his life for My sake will find it" (Matthew 16:25). That means if we want to have a life that is secure in the Lord, we have to let go of *our* plans and say, "Not my will, but *Yours* be done, Lord."

JULY 29

*T*hank You, Lord, that Your plans for my life are good, and You have a future for me that is full of hope. Thank You that You are always restoring my life to greater wholeness. I praise You and thank You that You are my Healer, my Deliverer, my Provider, my Redeemer, my Father, and my Comforter.

JUNE 5

*B*ut you are a chosen generation, a royal priesthood, a holy nation, His own special people, that you may proclaim the praises of Him who called you out of darkness into His marvelous light.

I Peter 2:9

*P*raising and worshiping God with other believers is one of the most powerfully significant things we can do in our lives. Corporate worship causes bondages to be broken, and it makes the way for wonderful changes in us that might never happen otherwise.

JUNE 6

*L*ord, help me to understand the call You have on my life. Take away any discouragement I may feel and replace it with joyful anticipation of what You are going to do through me. Use me as Your instrument to make a positive difference in the lives of those whom You put in my path.

JULY 27

*L*ord, forgive me when I neglect to praise and worship You as You deserve and desire. Teach me to worship You with my whole heart the way You want me to. Make me a *true* worshiper, Lord. May praise and worship of You be my first response to every circumstance.

JUNE 7

$\mathcal{W}$e all want to accomplish something significant with our lives. And we all have the potential to do something great. That's because we are the Lord's and His Spirit dwells in us. Because of His greatness *in* us, He can accomplish great things *through* us. When you know you are the Lord's and you trust where He is taking you, you feel very secure.

I will praise You with my whole heart; before the gods I will sing praises to You. I will worship toward Your holy temple, and praise Your name for Your loving kindness and Your truth; for You have magnified Your word above all Your name. In the day when I cried out, You answered me, and made me bold with strength in my soul.

PSALM 138:1-3

JUNE 8

*L*ord, help me to live my life with a sense of purpose and understanding of the calling You have given me. I lay down all pride, selfishness, and anything else that would keep me from moving into all You have for me.

JULY 25

*I*t doesn't matter if your work is recognized by the whole world or only God sees it. It doesn't matter if you are getting paid big bucks or receiving no financial compensation whatsoever. Your work is valuable. And you want it to be blessed by God.

JUNE 9

*W*alk worthy of the calling with which you were called, with all lowliness and gentleness, with longsuffering, bearing with one another in love, endeavoring to keep the unity of the Spirit in the bond of peace.

EPHESIANS 4:1-3

JULY 24

*L*ord, I pray You would show me what work I am supposed to be doing. If it is something I am to do in addition to what I am already doing, show me that too.

And let the beauty of the Lord our God be upon us, and establish the work of our hands for us; yes, establish the work of our hands.

PSALM 90:17

JUNE 10

*P*redestination means your destination has already been determined. The Bible says we are predestined according to God's purposes and will (Ephesians 1:11). That means God knows where you are supposed to be going. And He knows how to get you there.

*W*hatever work we do, we want to do it well and be successful. When our work is good, it gives us fulfillment. When we accomplish something worthwhile that makes life better for other people, our families, or ourselves, it gives us satisfaction.

JUNE 11

*L*ord, I thank You that You have called me with a holy calling, and I have a purpose because you have a plan for my life. I know that Your plan for me existed before I knew You, and You will bring it to pass.

JULY 22

$\mathcal{L}$ord, whatever it is You have called me to do, both now and in the future, I pray You will give me the strength and energy to get it done well. Enable me to do what I do successfully. May I find great fulfillment and satisfaction in every aspect of it, even the most difficult and unpleasant parts.

*G*od wants you to have a clear vision for your life. He wants to reveal to you what your gifts and talents are and show you how to best develop them and use them for His glory.

$\mathcal{P}$ray that your work is recognized and appreciated by others. Pray to receive promotions and advancement in line with God's will. Say, "Lord, I would like to have that promotion and that raise if it's Your will for my life." As you pray that way and commit your work to the Lord, He will bless it.

A highway shall be there, and a road, and it shall be called the Highway of Holiness.... The redeemed shall walk there, and the ransomed of the Lord shall return, and come to Zion with singing, with everlasting joy on their heads. They shall obtain joy and gladness, and sorrow and sighing shall flee away.

Isaiah 35:8,10

JULY 20

*T*hank You, Lord, that in all labor there is profit of one kind or another (Proverbs 14:23). I pray that the rewards of my work will be great. May I always be compensated fairly and richly out of the storehouse of Your abundance.

JUNE 14

$\mathcal{L}$ord, I know that You have called me to purity and holiness, and You have said that "He who calls you is faithful, who also will do it" (I Thessalonians 5:24). Thank You that You will keep me pure and holy so I will be fully prepared for all You have for me.

Just as He chose us in Him before the foundation of the world, that we should be holy and without blame before Him in love.

EPHESIANS 1:4

JULY 19

No matter what your paycheck reflects, your work is important to God, it's important to others, and it's important to you. You can't afford not to pray about it. Commit your work to the Lord and ask Him to bless it.

JUNE 15

*G*od wants to know that His holiness is important enough to us to seek after it. People are drawn to holiness because it is attractive, even though they may resist it on their own. Ask God to enhance your beauty with the beauty of His holiness.

*L*ord, I thank You for the abilities You have given me. Where I am lacking in skill, help me to grow and improve so that I do my work well. Teach me to excel so that the result of what I do will be pleasing to others.

JUNE 16

God has made a way for us to live in holiness. And He is able to *keep* us holy. When our heart wants to live in purity and do the right thing, God will keep us from falling into sin. It is only by the grace of God that we can live in holiness, even after we have chosen to do so. That's because God enables us to do what He asks us to do. But we still need to *ask* Him to do it.

JULY 17

I commit my work to You, Lord, knowing You will establish it (Proverbs 16:3). May it always be that I love the work I do and be able to do the work I love.

JUNE 17

*L*ord, enable me to do what it takes to get everything rooted out of my life that is not Your best for me so I can live the way You want me to live. Help me to examine my ways so that I can return to Your ways wherever I have strayed. Enable me to take any steps necessary in order to be pure before You.

Therefore, having these promises, beloved, let us cleanse ourselves from all filthiness of the flesh and spirit, perfecting holiness in the fear of God.

2 CORINTHIANS 7:1

JULY 16

*B*lessed is every one who fears the Lord, who walks in His ways. When you eat the labor of your hands, you shall be happy, and it shall be well with you.

PSALM 128:1-2

JUNE 18

*H*oliness is not something you slip in and out of like a nightgown. Holiness is God's will for our lives and something God has planned for us from the beginning.

Just as He chose us in Him before the foundation of the world, that we should be holy and without blame before Him in love, having predestined us to adoption as sons by Jesus Christ to Himself, according to the good pleasure of His will.

EPHESIANS 1:4–5

JULY 15

$\mathcal{L}$ord, according to Your Word I pray that I will not lag in diligence in my work, but remain fervent in spirit, serving You in everything I do (Romans 12:11). Establish the work of my hands so that what I do will find favor with others and be a blessing for many. May it always be glorifying to You.

Do you see a man who excels in his work? He will stand before kings; he will not stand before unknown men.

PROVERBS 22:29

JUNE 19

*E*steeming the holiness of God and living in purity is the only way we are able to be close to God. There is nothing more important than being close to Him.

By those who come near Me I must be regarded as holy; and before all the people I must be glorified.

LEVITICUS 10:3

*A*ll of us are planting something in our lives every *single* day, whether we realize it or not. And we are also reaping whatever we have planted in the past. The quality of our lives right now is the result of what we planted and harvested some time before.

JUNE 20

*L*ord, help me to separate myself from anything that is not holy. I don't want to waste my life on things that have no value. Give me discernment to recognize that which is worthless and remove myself from it. Help me not to give myself to impure things, but rather to those things that fulfill Your plans for my life.

JULY 13

*J*esus said that He is the vine and you and I are the branches. If we abide in Him we will bear fruit (John 15:5). "Abide" means to remain, to stay, to dwell. In other words, if we dwell with Him and He dwells with us, we will bear the fruit of His Spirit (Galatians 5:22-23). That's what we want.

JUNE 21

*T*he greatest lie our society has blindly accepted is that sexual sin is okay. It must grieve the Holy Spirit to see how women sell themselves short of all God has for them because they have bought into this lie. Holiness means not falling prey to fashion or trends of thought or deed. Ask God to keep you sexually pure in your mind, soul, and body.

JULY 12

*L*ord, search my heart and try me and see if there is any wickedness in me. Replace all that is wrong in my character with the goodness in Yours. Plant the fruit of Your Spirit in me and cause it to flourish.

But the fruit of the Spirit is love, joy, peace, longsuffering, kindness, goodness, faithfulness, gentleness, self-control. Against such there is no law.

GALATIANS 5:22-23

JUNE 22

*H*oliness means living in the Spirit and not in the flesh. Pray that God will help you live in the Spirit and not the flesh.

For those who live according to the flesh set their minds on the things of the flesh, but those who live according to the Spirit, the things of the Spirit.

ROMANS 8:5

JULY 11

*W*hen we share our lives with Jesus, His likeness is stamped on our spirit and soul. When we plug into Him, the fruit of His Spirit is manifested in us.

JUNE 23

$\mathcal{C}$ontinue to purify me by the power of Your Spirit, Lord. Help me to "cling to what is good" (Romans 12:9) and keep myself pure (1 Timothy 5:22).

JULY 10

*A*sk God to plant His love in you in such a profound and powerful way that you are able to fully experience it. Ask also that His love will flow through you to others.

JUNE 24

*W*hen God said, "Be holy" (Leviticus 19:2), He meant we are to take specific steps to see that we do not live an impure lifestyle. We are to deliberately turn away from anything that glorifies immorality and other unholiness.

But as He who called you is holy, you also be holy in all your conduct, because it is written, "Be holy, for I am holy."

1 PETER 1:15-16

JULY 9

*H*elp me abide in You, Jesus, so that I will bear fruit in my life. I invite You, Holy Spirit, to fill me afresh with Your love today so that it will flow out of me and into the lives of others.

JUNE 25

*L*ord, You have said in Your Word that You did not call me to uncleanness, but in holiness (1 Thessalonians 4:7). You chose me to be holy and blameless before you. I know that I have been washed clean and made holy by the blood of Jesus.

But you were washed, but you were sanctified, but you were justified in the name of the Lord Jesus and by the Spirit of our God.

1 CORINTHIANS 6:11

JULY 8

*J*esus said, "These things I have spoken to you, that My joy may remain in you, and that your joy may be full" (John 15:11). When you live in the joy of the Lord, you have expectations that God is going to do something great in your life. Pray for the joy of the Lord to be so planted *in* you and manifested *through* you that the crop you reap will spread and overtake the fields around you.

JUNE 26

$\mathcal{P}$urifying yourself means asking God, who is holy, to purify your heart. Unholiness happens there first. Purifying ourselves means taking stock of our lives, thoughts, actions, associations, and business dealings, and cleansing ourselves from anything that contaminates us.

And everyone who has this hope in Him purifies himself, just as He is pure.

1 John 3:3

JULY 7

"*The* peace of God, which surpasses all understanding, will guard your hearts and minds through Christ Jesus" (Philippians 4:7). We can only have true peace if we live in right relationship to God. Pray that God will help you to know His peace in such a powerful way that it brings peace to those around you.

JUNE 27

*B*eing holy is not being perfect. It's letting *Him* who is holy be *in* you. We can't be holy on our own, but we can make choices that allow holiness and purity to be manifested in our lives.

JULY 6

*W*hy do you think it's important to God that patience be growing in us? It's because God's timing is not our timing. He is always doing more than we see or know, so we have to trust Him on how long He takes to bring things to pass. God perfects and refines us before He brings us into all He has for us, and that takes time.

Where I need to be pruned in order to bear more fruit, Lord, I commit myself to You. I know that without You I can do nothing. You are the vine and I am the branch. I must abide in You in order to bear fruit. Help me to do that. Thank You for Your promise that if I abide in You and Your Word abides in me, I can ask what I desire and it will be done for me.

If you abide in Me, and My words abide in you, you will ask what you desire, and it shall be done for you. By this My Father is glorified, that you bear much fruit; so you will be My disciples.

JOHN 15:7-8

JULY 5

"*By* your patience possess your souls" (Luke 21:19). Another word for patience is longsuffering. And that says it all. When you suffer for a long time, it means you put up with more than you want to. Pray for God's patience to so be established in your soul that nothing you have to put up with will ever uproot it.

JUNE 29

"*A*dd to your faith virtue, to virtue knowledge, to knowledge self-control, to self-control perseverance, to perseverance godliness" (2 Peter 1:5-6). Ask God to plant self-control in you that will grow up like a tree of strength. Ask Him to help you rein in your passions, desires, and emotions to make them subject to His Spirit. He will give you the self-discipline you need.

JULY 4

*K*indness is something you choose to put on, like a garment. The ultimate act of kindness was when Jesus gave His life for us. Pray that His brand of kindness will grow in you so that you can lay down your life for others with acts of kindness too.

JUNE 30

*G*entleness is a humble meekness that is calm, soothing, peaceful, and easy to be around. Being considerate of the feelings and needs of others by exhibiting gentleness shows you are responding to the Spirit of God and what has been planted in you has taken root. Pray that you can be as gentle and meek as Jesus (2 Corinthians 10:1).

JULY 3

*L*ord, You said in Your Word to "let the peace of Christ rule in your hearts" (Colossians 3:15). I pray that Your *peace* would rule my heart and mind to such a degree that people would sense it when they are around me.

JULY 1

When we are solid, steadfast, dependable, reliable, loyal, and trustworthy and do what is right no matter what, we exhibit faithfulness. Pray that His faithfulness will continually grow strong in every day you are alive. Pray that your faithfulness will strengthen everyone you touch and inspire others to greater faithfulness too.

JULY 2